TINKER and the Medicine Men

Tinker Yazzie is a boy with a special heritage. Not only is he a Navajo Indian, but he is the son and grandson of medicine men. He wants to become a medicine man, too.

With spectacular photographs and a sensitive text, Bernard Wolf portrays one week in Tinker's life—the exciting week he returns home to Monument Valley, Arizona, after spending the school year in town.

In between the daily activities of his family—watering the flocks, shearing sheep, weaving rugs—Tinker receives his first formal lessons in the ways of a medicine man. His father begins to teach him about the practices of the traditional Navajo "singer," and about the newer ways of the peyote religion. At the end of the busy week, Tinker participates in a peyote ceremony for the first time.

Tinker and the Medicine Men captures another way of life in America—and shows the many-sided education of one Navajo boy.

TINKER
and the Medicine Men

THE STORY OF A NAVAJO BOY OF MONUMENT VALLEY

written and photographed by Bernard Wolf

Random House 🏠 New York

The author wishes to thank Mr. Evan Roberts, formerly of the Office of Navajo Economic Opportunity, Fort Defiance, Arizona, for his consistent encouragement; Mr. Sam Day III, Assistant Director, Resources Division, Navajo Tribe, for his enthusiastic support during the initial stages of preparing this book; and Mr. Bill Crawley, Golden Sands Tours, Kayenta, Arizona, whose generous help made this book possible. Most of all, great thanks are due to Mr. Tony Yazzie and all the members of his family in Monument Valley, who accepted the author on faith and taught him the true meaning of kindness, patience, and understanding.

Library of Congress Cataloging in Publication Data: Wolf, Bernard. Tinker and the medicine men. Summary: Follows the activities of Tinker's Navajo family the week he finishes first grade, moves for the summer to his ancestral home in Monument Valley, and begins studying to be a medicine man. 1.Navajo Indians—Juvenile Literature. [1.Navajo Indians.] I.Title   E99.N3W73   970.3[B]   72-11058   ISBN 0-394-82360-5   ISBN 0-394-92360-X (lib. bdg.)

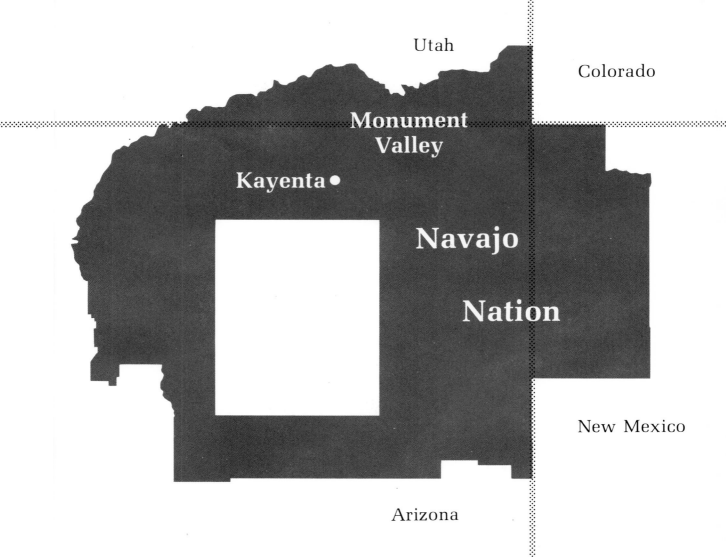

Utah

Colorado

Monument Valley

Kayenta ●

Navajo

Nation

New Mexico

Arizona

This book is gratefully dedicated to the People of the Valley. May you always wander with beauty.

Tinker Yazzie is a Navajo Indian boy with a difficult ambition. He wants to become a medicine man like his father and grandfathers. Although he is only six years old, he is not too young to decide. He has already shown that he has an excellent memory, loves to learn new things, and has great self-discipline— qualities he will need in the long years of study ahead.

Medicine men are very important to the Navajos. They are responsible for curing their people's physical and mental ailments. If they are traditional medicine men, they also help to preserve the Navajos' ancient religious beliefs and values. If they are peyote chiefs of the Native American Church, they help the peyote worshipers to find new strength to deal with the problems of changing times. Tinker's father is unusual—he is both kinds of medicine man.

Tinker's tribe was given the name Navajo by the Spaniards who came to the Southwest in the seventeenth century. In their own language, the Navajos call themselves "Diné"—the People.

The ways of the People are changing. Though they are many, they are but an island surrounded by a sea of white men. Though they wish to keep their old beliefs and traditions, they have learned that in order to survive they must adapt to the ways of the more powerful white society in America.

Tinker knows that his first task is to learn English. At home he speaks Navajo. For him, English is a foreign language taught at school.

Tinker attends the public school in Kayenta, Arizona. Today he is finishing first grade. Tomorrow he will return to his ancestral home in Monument Valley for the summer.

Tinker spends his last afternoon in school on reading and arithmetic lessons. The class practices adding and subtracting with piles of shells that their teacher, Mrs. Wilson, counts out for them.

Mrs. Wilson then passes out her parting gifts to the class—drawing paper and new boxes of crayons. She asks the children to draw her a picture while she makes out their report cards. Tinker soon shows her a drawing of his home in Monument Valley.

"Who's that man on the horse?" asks Mrs. Wilson.

"That's my brother Wilbart. He's riding the black pony my father just gave him for his birthday. Wilbart's eight. He's going to be a rodeo rider," Tinker announces proudly.

Mrs. Wilson admires the picture and then gives Tinker his final report card. Tinker studies it thoughtfully. Next to every subject on his card is a check mark for "excellent." He doesn't say anything except to thank his teacher. Among the Navajos, it is considered bad manners to show too much pride in oneself. Still, Tinker is quietly pleased.

The schoolbell rings, setting off a terrific commotion throughout the building. Students call good-bye to teachers and friends, and parents arrive to pick up their children. Tinker's father appears at the door of the classroom.

"How's my boy been doing?" asks Tony Yazzie.

"Just fine," says Mrs. Wilson. "You can be proud of Tinker. And please tell your wife we've had no problems at all with Tinker's hair."

Tinker is the first Navajo boy in his school to be allowed to keep his hair long in the traditional manner. Tinker and his parents requested special permission because of Tinker's strong religious beliefs, and the principal agreed.

Tinker and Tony say good-bye to Mrs. Wilson and go off to get Wilbart, who is in second grade in the same school. Tony decides to give the boys a special treat—a visit to the soda fountain at the big Holiday Inn in town.

Tinker and Wilbart order double chocolate ice cream sundaes with lots of syrup and whipped cream. They dig in eagerly, but before long Tinker loses enthusiasm and stops eating. He is not used to the feeling of so much cold stuff going down into his belly. Soon Wilbart stops eating too.

The boys don't say anything. They don't have to. Their father understands and calmly finishes their sundaes for them. Tinker and Wilbart know that their father doesn't like ice cream. This is his way of silently telling them that wastefulness is not acceptable. They will remember this lesson without being embarrassed by it.

Tony Yazzie has a good, year-round job in Kayenta. He works as a tour driver and guide, showing visitors to his nation some of the wonders of the Navajo wildlands.

During the winter months, the Yazzie family lives in a trailer in Kayenta so that the boys can go to school in town. Otherwise the children would have to go away to a boarding school run by the Bureau of Indian Affairs. Tony is grateful that he can spare his boys this separation from the family. One of Tinker's cousins went away to school this year and found it a painful and lonely experience.

While the Yazzies live in town, Tony's mother-in-law remains behind at

their home in Monument Valley, looking after the family's dwellings and live-stock. But with the coming of spring, there is far too much work for one woman alone. Tony's wife, Rose, went back to help her mother a few weeks ago, taking the three youngest children with her. Now Tony is taking a week off from his job to help the family get settled for the summer.

Late in the afternoon Tony and the boys return to the trailer. While Tony prepares a light supper, Tinker makes some more pictures with the paper and crayons that his teacher gave him. The boys go to bed before sundown and soon fall fast asleep. Tomorrow will be a long and exciting day.

Everyone gets up at 4:00 the next morning and eats a quick breakfast. By dawn they are on their way in Tony's pickup truck. Wilbart curls up in the back for a nap, but Tinker hangs over the front seat. He is eager to see his mother again and to taste his grandmother's good homecooking.

The Yazzie home is thirty-five miles north of Kayenta. Tony drives the first twenty-five miles on a modern highway and soon arrives at the edge of Monument Valley. The scene before them is that of a fierce, unyielding land, unfertile and hostile to all forms of life. But in this unfriendly landscape there is also a wild and awesome beauty which the Navajos love. This is Tinker's true home.

There are no roads in the Valley—only steep, winding paths covered with sand and shale. This is some of the roughest terrain in the Southwest. But Tony knows the land well and is an excellent driver.

Tony is returning to a land beset with problems. There is a terrible drought in the Navajo Nation. For more than eight months there has been no rain. The People are very worried. Monument Valley is always an extremely arid region, and now, most of the Valley's washes and waterholes are drying up. There is even less vegetation than usual, and many sheep are dying of hunger and thirst.

At last Tony drives up to the family hogan. Tinker's mother and two young sisters come out to greet them.

Tinker murmurs the traditional Navajo greeting, "Yah teh!"

"Yah teh!" says Rose, smiling. "It is good that we are all together again. Come into the hogan."

Tony built this hogan himself. It took him three months, using an axe as his only tool. The hogan is dome-shaped, about twenty feet in diameter. It consists of a framework of juniper logs covered with eight inches of juniper bark and plastered on the outside with a foot of adobe (sun-dried clay). The only openings are a smoke hole in the roof and a door, which by custom faces east toward the rising sun. Because of its thick, well-insulated wall, the hogan can be heated efficiently in winter with a small amount of firewood. During the intensely hot summers in the Valley, the temperature is always much lower in the hogan.

Inside, they are greeted by Tinker's grandmother, Bessie Jones Black. At the sight of Tinker, she hugs his two-year-old sister, Mary Rose, with pleasure. She will not embarrass Tinker by hugging him in front of the others.

"Yah teh, Mother," Tinker greets her. Among the Navajos, all aunts and grandmothers are called mother.

Rose notices that Tinker's long hair has not been bound up, and she swiftly fixes it. What would people in Kayenta think if they saw her son so carelessly groomed? Tony reassures her that they left town too early to be seen by anyone.

Everyone starts exchanging news of the Valley and Kayenta. Since there are no telephones in the Valley and the family has been separated for weeks, there is much news to catch up on.

After a while, Tinker's grandmother leaves the hogan and goes to a small shack nearby. Here she begins to mix dough for fried bread. With it she will serve a large pot of mutton stew, which has been simmering outside over a slow fire since early morning. She asks Wilbart to chop some more wood for her.

Then Tinker's grandmother builds another fire and fries the pancake-shaped bread in a heavy iron skillet. She does all her cooking outdoors in hot weather to avoid extra heat in the hogan.

By noon the food is ready. Rose lays a clean cloth on the sand floor of the hogan and helps place the food on it. Everyone sits comfortably in a circle and begins to eat. As an extra treat, there is jelly for the bread and a can of Spam. There are also cans of Coke, 7 Up, and Pepsi Cola.

Though he is soon full, Tinker can hardly stop eating. Looking about him, he sighs with contentment. He is happy to be home and in a hogan once more.

After their meal, all the children take a nap. Tony rests for a little while but he has no time to sleep. He must help shear the sheep this week. Soon he quietly slips down to the corral and begins the hot, strenuous work.

About an hour later, Tinker shows up at the corral rubbing the sleep out of his eyes and asking if he can help.

"Come and hold this sheep's head for me, if you like. Watch what I do so that you'll know how to do it yourself when the time comes," replies Tony.

He has thrown the sheep on its side and tied its legs together to prevent being kicked by the animal. Now, with a heavy pair of shears, he carefully cuts the fleece from the sheep's hide in a long, even line, rolling the wool back like a thick blanket.

When he finishes shearing each animal, Tony shakes the wool free of dust and puts it aside. Later he'll pack the wool into large sacks. The Yazzies sell about 300 pounds of wool each year for thirty-five cents a pound. They keep twenty to thirty pounds of wool for Rose and her mother to weave into rugs.

Tinker wants to see if he can shear too. He grabs a small black lamb and throws it to the ground. Then he ties its legs. The shears are too big and heavy for him to handle but he is determined to try. Tony knows that Tinker will not hurt the lamb, and he murmurs a few words of direction and encouragement.

In the hogan, Rose tries to interest her daughter in the rug that she is weaving. Mary Rose likes to touch the strands on the loom, but she soon becomes restless. Rose takes the loom outside where she can work and watch her daughter play at the same time.

Navajo rugs are among the finest woven products of all the Indian tribes of North America. No two are ever exactly alike. The weaver never prepares a pattern.

Rose weaves ten rugs every year. Each takes her a month to complete. She could weave more but, like many of her people, she believes that moderation in all things is best. She spends no more than two hours at weaving each day.

The excellent quality of her rugs brings Rose more acclaim and better prices every year, but she fears too much fame or perfection. For hundreds of years, the People have believed in the wisdom of this fear. And so, in each rug she weaves, Rose makes sure to include some small imperfection—some slight, irregular opening in an edge of the design to release the envy of evil spirits.

Rose tells her husband that his old aunt Many Goats has been complaining of poor health lately. Good health is a constant matter of concern to all Navajos—particularly to Tony Yazzie, since he is both a peyote chief and a Navajo medicine man.

Later that afternoon Tony and Tinker drive ten miles to where Tony's aunt lives in the Valley. Aunt Many Goats is a 68-year-old widow. Her late husband built the house where she lives with Tony's sister. In spite of her advanced age, she is a valuable and respected member of her large family. She still works very hard looking after all the sheep and goats that belong to her and Tony's sister.

Tony asks what ails her.

"Ah," she says softly, "my joints burn as if they are on fire. Sometimes, after driving the flock back from the watering place, I can barely get off my horse."

Tony listens with concern. After a moment's silence, Many Goats asks, "Do you think, my son, that we could hold a peyote ceremony soon? I believe that the good powers of King Peyote will come to my aid now as before."

A peyote ceremony requires a lot of planning and expense, but Tony agrees immediately. "Mother, my thoughts walk with yours. The time is good. Next Saturday marks the birth of the new moon. Also, it is a good time to begin instructing Tinker in the way of the Peyote Trail. I will place his feet upon it and try to guide him. Now let me see what can be done."

Tony and Tinker drive over to John Simpson's place. John is Tony's half brother. He and his family are the Yazzies' closest neighbors, living only one mile away. He has recently built a breezy summer shed by his hogan.

The two men discuss Many Goats, and then John reports that his wife has been troubled by terrible fears and bad dreams. He is worried that a spell has been cast on her by some unknown Navajo witch or an evil spirit. He is eager to help organize a peyote ceremony for the two women and offers the use of his new summer shed on Saturday night.

When they return home, Tony takes Tinker to the corral and saddles up his horse, Billie.

"We have many important things to discuss," he says. "Let us begin by riding out to the place of the Anasazi. The noise of a car engine is not suitable for serious thought."

Tinker rides behind Tony on the horse, holding tightly to his father's waist. He looks nervously at the ground. Like all Navajos, Tinker loves horses; but he hasn't learned to ride yet. Because Tony spends most of the year in town, he hasn't had a chance to teach Tinker.

With the sun low on the horizon, all the fantastic sandstone shapes around them glow with an eerie light. They ride slowly across the floor of the Valley. Beyond them stand the Yeibichai Dancers and the nearly 500-foot-tall Totem Pole—huge rock formations that are sacred to the People of the Valley. These and other wind-sculpted rocks, which look like ancient monuments, gave the Valley its name.

Tinker wonders if his father is going to explain some of the peyote mysteries to him now. Tinker has attended peyote ceremonies before, but never as a full participant. There is much that he does not understand. He would like to question his father, but he has been trained never to press a subject through his own impatience. Tony will talk when he feels that the time is right.

Tony and Tinker ride up to Echo Cave. There they dismount and sit contemplating the sight before them. Cut into the side of a huge mesa are old dwellings. These are some of the remains of the Anasazi—the Ancient Ones—cliff dwellers who lived in this part of the country almost a thousand years ago. Many Navajos fear the evil spirits of the dead Anasazi in this place. Tony, however, does not.

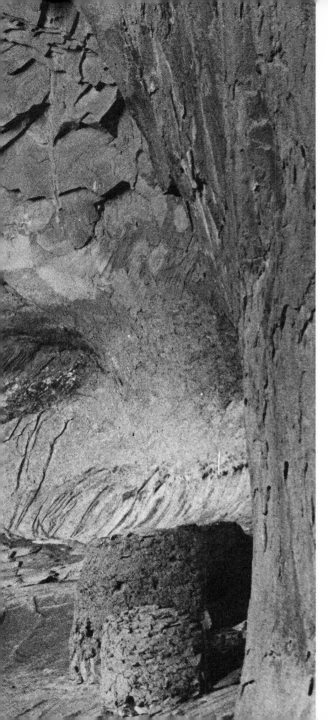

Tony breaks the vast silence. "Look well upon these ruins of a once peaceful and prosperous people."

"What happened to them?"

"They were probably destroyed by other people," answers Tony.

"But why would anyone want to destroy them if they were peaceful?"

"Maybe," Tony replies, "because the Anasazi medicine was different from theirs. Sometimes, what men do not understand, they fear. Often, the things they fear they attempt to destroy. Our old ways are good, but even now there are some among the People who are against the Peyote Way. They say bad things about it because it is new to them. I have tested King Peyote's powers for many years. He has brought me new strength. I accept his truth as I accept the truths of our ancient gods. It is foolish to throw away a thing without first testing it to see if there is good in it."

Sensing that Tony is not ready to say any more, Tinker says, "I will think carefully about your words, Father."

"Good," replies Tony. "We will speak about this again. Now, let us ride home before night falls."

Early the next morning Tony says to Tinker, "It is time to test your endurance. This morning you alone will take the sheep and goats to water at Sand Springs. Are you willing?"

The Navajos believe that as soon as a boy can understand and is physically fit, he should be given tests to prepare him for life's hardships. At the same time, no one is asked to take such a test against his will.

"I am willing," Tinker replies, and follows his father to the corral.

Tinker's trial will not be an easy one. It is five miles to Sand Springs.

"Try to keep the flock together and moving at a good pace until you bring them to water," Tony instructs him. "Speed is important. The animals must return before the sun makes the ground too hot for their soft feet. The dogs will help you, and I will follow behind on horseback in case you have trouble."

Tony nods at Tinker and pulls open the corral gate. Tinker picks up a piece of rope. With a loud cry, he dashes into the corral, swinging the rope in a circle to drive the flock out through the gate.

This takes courage. Most of the animals are bigger than he is, and some of the goats have dangerous-looking horns.

Once outside the corral, Tinker begins to enjoy his trial. The flock runs swiftly before him up the rise toward the big mesa that guards the approach to Sand Springs.

When the Spaniards introduced sheep and goats to the Indians of the Southwest, they changed the Navajos' way of life. Before that, the Navajos had been hunters and gatherers of wild nuts, fruits, and grains. After they began to raise their own livestock, their food supply became more secure and their prosperity increased.

But the Navajos paid a high price for what at first seemed a blessing. Sheep and goats need much space to graze in and must often be moved to new areas to allow the cropped plants to regrow. As the land-hungry white settlers moved westward in the nineteenth century, they seized the Indians' best grazing lands. Today much of the remaining Navajo land is dead or dying from overgrazing and soil erosion.

Tinker takes the flock past the big mesa. He has one more mile to go before reaching water. He finds it harder to walk now because here the Valley floor is thickly covered with sand. He is getting very tired, and the most difficult stretch still lies before him. But he is afraid that if he stops to rest he may not be able to continue.

With a burst of determination, he lets out another loud yell and throws handfuls of sand at the animals. They begin to run. Soon they are crossing the steep sand dunes which roll like red-gold hills on both sides of the springs. Tinker finds the dunes hard to climb but he has fun sliding down them.

There is only one more sand dune to climb and there below, like a slender silver thread, lies Sand Springs. The flock runs thirstily toward the water.

The water comes from five feet below the sand and rock. Because of the drought, the supply this year is very low. Unfortunately, the water at Sand Springs is too alkaline for people to drink safely. The Yazzies' own supply must be hauled in from a fresh-water well fifteen miles away.

Tony rides up smiling and says, "You have done well, Tinker."

Tony and Tinker sit down together to wait for the animals to finish drinking. "In my father's time," Tony remarks, "these sand dunes were just beginning to form. Most of this land still held good, rich buffalo grass, buckwheat, and wildflowers; all gone. The earth is tired now. I think that soon our people will no longer be able to depend on their livestock to support them."

"How will we live without our sheep and goats?" exclaims Tinker.

"We will have to learn new ways."

"Is that why you are pleased that I am going to the white man's school and learning English?"

"Yes," says Tony. "I am equally pleased that you want to become a medicine man. Too many of our younger generation are forsaking the ways of the People. Their minds and spirits are troubled. They are neither Navajo nor white and they become strangers to both."

"Then why do you want me to learn the white man's ways, Father?"

"Because both paths will help you to help your people. The white men are many and they will not go away. The better we understand their ways, the more easily we can deal with them as equals.

"You know," Tony continues with a hint of a smile, "when God decided to create man, he built an oven and made some clay figures. He made a fire in the oven and put the first figure inside. When he took it out, the man was a yellow color. 'Not baked enough,' God said. He put another clay figure in the oven and brought out a black man. 'Cooked too long,' God said. The next clay figure came out a nice, reddish-brown color. 'That's just right!' said God. He had one white clay figure left. But by this time, he was too tired to bake any more so he just blew on it to give it life. Maybe that's why the white man has never been satisfied with anything," concludes Tony with a straight face.

Tinker roars with laughter as Tony hoists him onto the horse for the trip home.

The following afternoon, Tony prepares to give Tinker his first lesson in the art of sand painting. This art is a traditional Navajo religious practice, and plays no part in the peyote religion.

Tony has collected the raw materials for the pigments he will need. From sandstone, he will make red and brown; from limestone, white. Yellow will come from crushed corn and black from wood charcoal. Mixing the charcoal with limestone will produce grey.

Tony carefully grinds each color on a flat rock. "Most of our great old singers have died," he says to Tinker.

The Navajos call their medicine men "singers" because of their mastery of the many complex songs and chants used in every traditional Navajo curing ceremony. During a ceremony, the sick person sits on a sand painting while the medicine man sings over him.

"Once, I too wanted to become a great singer," Tony continues, "but I began my training too late. My knowledge is limited. I will teach you what I know. Later, if you want to learn more, you will have to be apprenticed to a more accomplished singer."

When Tony's pigments are ready, he clears a large space and pours a heap of clean, neutral-colored sand on the ground. With his wife's weaving stick, he smooths the sand into a flat, four-foot circle. This will be the background for his painting.

"Our people do not use a written language to preserve our ancient knowledge," says Tony. "What I know, I have learned by watching carefully and by remembering exactly what I have been taught by other singers. You will have to do the same, Tinker. A singer cannot make any errors. The gods do not forget or forgive easily. When we sing over a patient, we call upon their powers to help us heal the afflicted one. The correct procedures and rules must be strictly followed. Otherwise, the cure will not work."

Tony is going to paint one of the sacred forms of the Yeibichai, a group of powerful Navajo gods. He first chants a special prayer to the Yeibichai, explaining why he is painting when there is no curing ceremony, and asking their forgiveness. Now he can safely begin.

Tony makes two guidelines on the sand with a string. Then he takes some ground limestone in his hand and slowly begins to paint the outline of a figure. With astonishing control, he lets just the right amount of pigment trickle out between his thumb and forefinger. At no time may his hand touch the surface of his painting. He is working entirely from memory, painting the figure exactly as he has been taught.

After a while, the sacred form appears. Tinker watches closely as his father begins to fill in some of the required designs on the figure, using the other pigments. When Yeibichai comes sufficiently to life in the painting, Tony starts to sing a wishing song. Tinker joins in.

In this song, man asks the Yeibichai to grant his wish. They agree to do so as long as man prays to them, with a clean mind, body, and heart. To make sure the Yeibichai will not forget their promise, man makes his request once more and receives the same response. Man is satisfied. The rules have been observed and there is harmony between man and god.

The painting is finished. Tinker silently studies the holy image.

A long, difficult trail lies ahead of Tinker. Although a singer is well paid for his services and is respected by his people, he must devote all his life to learning and using his knowledge well.

If, among the many Navajo ceremonies, Tinker chooses to study a four-night sing, he will just be starting to learn the appropriate chants, prayers, and rituals when he is twenty. If he wants to specialize in the longest ceremony of all—the nine-night sing, he may be in his forties before he has learned it.

Tinker will have to master the technique for painting the large, intricate figures that each ceremony requires. He will have to learn to seat his patients correctly on his paintings, to diagnose their problems accurately, and to choose the most helpful treatment. He will have to learn how to use medicinal herbs. Above all, he must never forget that the gift of life is a sacred blessing which he must help preserve.

Tony picks up the weaving stick once more. "The painting has done its work well," he says. "I am pleased. Now we must give it back." He slowly erases the painting in the same order in which it was made. He prays to the Yeibichai, thanking them for their help and asking them to keep away bad spirits. Then he gathers up the sand containing the used pigments, takes it outside, and returns the elements to the earth from where they came.

Tinker asks his father if he can try painting too. Tony smooths some fresh sand onto the ground. Then he takes the boy's hand and shows him how to adjust his thumb and forefinger for the best control of the pigment. Tinker tries to duplicate the Yeibichai figure but he soon discovers just how difficult it is. After a while, he also finds that the position for painting puts a strain on his body.

"Don't be discouraged," says Tony. "That's not so bad for a start. You should have seen *my* first attempt. It was awful! We have done enough now."

For the next few days, Tony says no more about the ways of a medicine man. Tinker is content simply to be at home and to play with his brothers and sisters. His parents and grandmother are kept busy with the rest of the sheep shearing. Tony also has many repair jobs to do before the week is up.

Late Friday afternoon Tony saddles up Billie and once more he and Tinker ride out into the Valley. This time Tony wears his best blanket and carries his peyote instrument box. Tinker knows that his patience is about to be rewarded. When they reach Sourdough Pass, they dismount and walk among the huge rocks.

"At Echo Cave we saw some of the works of man," says Tony. "This is a good place to study some of the works of God. This will remain long after we are gone."

"But there's nothing here but a lot of big, dead rocks," says Tinker.

"How can you be sure they are dead?" asks his father. "How can you be sure that they don't live and breathe and have a spirit of their own, different from ours?"

Tony next takes Tinker to North Window, one of his favorite spots in the Valley. Here he says, "I have spent my life seeking out those trails which bring me closer to God. One of the paths I have chosen to follow is the Peyote Way. When you are older, you will have to choose for yourself the path that is best for you."

Tony opens his instrument box and shows Tinker the objects inside. Among them is a small, heavy silver box, which he holds with reverence.

"All over the world, men speak to different gods in different tongues and call them by different names. There is wisdom and truth to be found in all those gods. But since I have started on the Peyote Trail, I have come to believe that there is really only one God for all men, whatever name we may give him."

Tony opens the silver box and passes it to Tinker. Lying inside is a dried, brown, vegetable-like object with some spiny hairs sticking out from the top. Tinker stares at it. It doesn't look very attractive. Thinking of the beautiful Navajo gods he has seen in sand paint-

ings, he looks at the thing in his hand and wonders what all the fuss is about.

"This is the Peyote King," says his father. "Handle him with respect, for he contains great powers."

"Is he a god?" asks Tinker.

"No. He is a key that unlocks a door to God and lets us see him more clearly."

"Where do his powers come from?"

"No one knows his secret, not even the scientists who have tried to discover it. We only know that when we eat his flesh and when we pray to him with pure hearts, then King Peyote allows us to see many wonderful truths."

"But what does he let us see?" asks Tinker.

"This cannot be described by words. Each of us has his own experience. What we see depends on what we are."

Tinker looks puzzled. His father smiles and says, "Perhaps you'll find out tomorrow night."

Tony takes a water-drum stick from the instrument box and gives it to Tinker to beat time with. As the sun sets, they sing a closing prayer to the end of day.

On Saturday, Tony goes to help with the preparations for that evening's ceremony. As the day passes, Tinker becomes both excited and nervous.

When Tony returns he takes Tinker to the sweatbath hogan. There he builds a fire and places large, flat stones around the flames to heat them. He and Tinker undress except for their breechcloths and moccasins. When the stones become hot, Tony shovels them into the hogan.

In a land where water is scarce, the sweatbath gives the People a natural way to keep their bodies clean. Its intense dry heat also eases tired or tense muscles. It has a religious use too; no Navajo singer would ever hold a curing ceremony without first purifying himself in a sweatbath. Likewise, Tony purifies himself before a peyote ceremony.

Once inside, Tony and Tinker sing four sweatbath songs. After an hour, they've had enough and dart out into the cool air. They dry themselves by rubbing sand on their bodies, and dress. Tinker has a new shirt and trousers for the ceremony, and Tony is wearing his best blue satin shirt.

About twenty-five members of the family clan have gathered at John Simpson's place. Outside the summer shed, Many Goats talks with the women who are busy preparing food for everyone. Tinker and Tony greet them and go on into the shed. Inside, brightly colored blankets decorate the walls. Sheepskins, clean sheets, mattresses, and cushions have been placed along the sides of the room for the worshipers to sit on.

The Yazzies sit down beside Oris Salazar, who will run this evening's ceremony so that Tony can instruct Tinker. Oris is Tony's brother-in-law. He is the only qualified peyote chief in the Valley besides Tony. It was Tony's father who, in 1930, introduced the peyote religion to the People of the Valley. He learned of it from a wandering Cheyenne medicine man who, in turn, had learned of it from the Indians of Mexico.

The ancient Aztecs were the first to discover the magic properties of a cactus plant that still grows in the northern deserts of Mexico. They called it "peyotl"—the flesh of the gods. By eating the dried tops of this plant, they experienced amazing visions and insights.

The ceremonial use of peyote has spread from the Indians of Mexico to many Indian tribes in the United States. Here it has become an organized practice under the Native American Church of North America. Many Navajos who have adopted the peyote religion continue to follow some of the traditional Navajo religious customs. Some also follow Christian practices.

While adults and children wander in and out chatting with each other, the summer shed is converted into a church. Many Goats comes in to watch while she shucks long ears of Indian corn for tomorrow morning's feast.

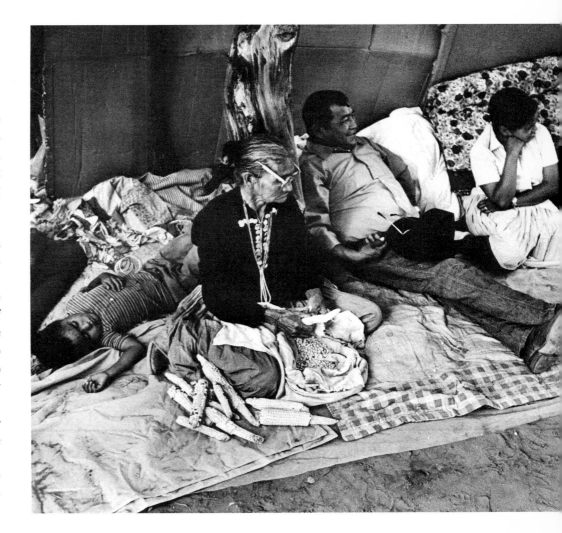

Near the middle of the room John Simpson builds the altar for the ceremony, shaping clean, wet sand into the form of a crescent. This represents the new moon—symbol of woman, fertility, and new life.

Next a water drum is made by stretching buckskin over a small cast-iron kettle half-filled with water. The drum will be used all through the ceremony to call God's attention to the worshipers. John Simpson will be the "drum man."

Stanley Jones, the "fire man," builds a fire which must be kept alive all night to discourage evil spirits.

The peyote chief now finishes the altar. Using his pocket comb, Oris Salazar inscribes a line along the top of the crescent. This represents the path of everlasting life. Then Oris arranges a small cushion of purifying sage leaves exactly on the center of the new moon and makes a wish for prosperity on a silver half-dollar.

Near the altar Tony sets down a jar of dried, ground peyote, a kettle of strong tea brewed from more peyote, and the water drum. The men sit back for a moment to make sure that nothing has been overlooked. They are satisfied.

Now the women bring in food. Everyone begins to eat hastily because the meal must be finished before sunset. This is the last food they will taste until late tomorrow morning. Tony urges his son to eat as much as he can, but for once Tinker's appetite has deserted him.

Outside, a line forms behind Oris Salazar, who holds the instrument box. The sun must see the worshipers before it sets so it can know that their purpose is a good one and give them its blessing. When it sinks below the horizon, everyone enters the church. They will not leave it again until sunrise, except for a short break at midnight.

By the time everyone is comfortably settled, darkness has fallen outside. In deep silence Oris Salazar brings forth the Peyote King from the heavy silver box.

Reverently placing the sacred button on the sage cushion, he prays for King Peyote's help during the long night ahead. He adds a handful of cedar chips to the fire to perfume the air. The ceremony has begun.

The adults roll cigarettes from loose store tobacco, puffing on them as a token of brotherhood and in remembrance of their forefathers who long ago smoked the peace pipe. Each smoker says a prayer. Tony prays for wisdom in guiding his son on the right path of knowledge. He and all the others pray for better health for John Simpson's wife, for Many Goats, and for all their relatives in the Valley.

The time for taking the peyote has come. The jar of ground peyote and the kettle are slowly passed clockwise. When they reach Tinker, Tony carefully measures out a half portion of peyote into the boy's hand. He tells him to chew it well and swallow. Tinker finds the taste terribly bitter but he wants to learn about peyote, so he swallows the stuff. He washes it down with a cup of peyote tea, which doesn't taste as bad.

After midnight, the peyote will be taken twice more.

Suddenly the silence is broken by the beat of the water drum and the high-pitched notes of a worshiper lifting his voice to God.

"Hear my voice! I listen to yours. I want to be with you. I will follow in your path. I love you. I love myself. I love the earth, I love the sky. Give me my good wishes! I will follow in your path."

He sings four songs in all, then passes the drum to the next person who wants to use it.

During the pause between singers, Oris Salazar throws more cedar chips on the fire and moves the smoke into the air with a feather fan to ward off evil spirits. He asks John Simpson's wife and Many Goats how they are feeling. Aunt Many Goats replies that her aches and pains are beginning to lessen. But John Simpson's wife says that she feels an evil presence outside their church. She fears they are being spied on by a Navajo witch!

At this news there is a gasp of alarm from all sides. Navajo witches are not to be taken lightly. They are people who practice evil arts against all the laws of god and man. Sometimes they appear wearing the skins of wolves or coyotes. Their powers for destruction are awesome.

Oris asks everyone to pray with him for protection and courage. He sings a special song of power against the dark forces while John Simpson plays the drum. But the feeling of uneasiness remains until past midnight.

After the peyote has been taken for the second time, a new atmosphere of serenity and hope envelopes the gathering. The throb of the drum becomes the steady beat of a strong heart. The light of the fire becomes a flood of illumination through which each worshiper sees God in his own way.

Long before dawn comes, Tinker falls into a deep sleep. He dreams that his spirit and his flesh have become part of the Valley that he loves so much. No matter where he may go or what he may do in later years, he knows he will have but one true home. And in his dream he hears his father's voice singing the words of an ancient Navajo song:

Beauty before me, with it I wander.
Beauty behind me, with it I wander.
Beauty below me, with it I wander.
Beauty above me, with it I wander.
Beauty all around me, with it I
wander.
In old age traveling, with it I
wander.
On the beautiful trail I am, with
it I wander.

About the Author

Bernard Wolf is a photographer with a remarkable ability to relate people to their environment. He has previously demonstrated this skill in three other books about children of other cultures: *Daniel and the Whale Hunters* (set in the Azores), *Jamaica Boy*, and *The Little Weaver of Agato* (set in Ecuador). In addition, Mr. Wolf's photographs have appeared in Time-Life books and in *Fortune, Camera 35*, and *Travel and Camera* magazines.

Mr. Wolf has led a varied life in his native city of New York. He began working as a professional singer at the age of eight. After graduation from the High School of Music and Art, he studied voice at Mannes College of Music, then turned to the field of interior design for ten years. He finally settled on photography, specializing in portraying peoples and cultures all over the world. He has traveled extensively ever since. When not on assignment, he and his wife, Ana, live in Manhattan.